MW01228016

Turn Your Ideas
Into Millions

Turn Your Ideas Into Millions

Selling and Marketing Your Idea or Product

Kate Masters

A Citadel Press Book

Published by Carol Publishing Group

Copyright © 1994 by Kate Masters

A Citadel Press Book
Published by Carol Publishing Group
Citadel Press is a registered trademark of Carol Communications, Inc.
Editorial Offices: 600 Madison Avenue, New York, N.Y. 10022
Sales and Distribution Offices: 120 Enterprise Avenue, Secaucus, N.J. 07094
In Canada: Canadian Manda Group, P.O. Box 920, Station U, Toronto, Ontario M8Z 5P9
Queries regarding rights and permissions should be addressed to Carol Publishing Group, 600 Madison Avenue, New York, N.Y. 10022

Carol Publishing Group books are available at special discounts for bulk purchases, for sales promotions, fund raising, or educational purposes. Special editions can be created to specifications.
For details contact: Special Sales Department, Carol Publishing Group, 120 Enterprise Avenue, Secaucus, N.J. 07094

Manufactured in the United States of America

10 9 8 7 6 5 4 3 2 1

Library of Congress Cataloging-in-Publication Data

Masters, Kate
   Turn your ideas into millions : selling and marketing your idea or product / by Kate Masters.
        p.   cm.
   "A Learning Annex book."
   "A Citadel Press book."
   ISBN 0-8065-1525-2
   1. New products—Management.   2. New products—Marketing.
I. Title.
HF5415.153.M34   1994
658.5'75—dc20   93-44225
                                                      CIP

Contents

PART III: *Producing and Manufacturing Your Idea*

PART V: *Expansion*

Part I

The First Steps: Evaluating, Protecting, and Developing Your Idea

1 | *Evaluating Your Idea*

Do you have a new idea for a product or service that you're excited about? That's great, but do you know what to do next? It takes time, commitment, and money, but by following the clear steps in this book, you will be able to turn your idea into reality.

You begin by evaluating your idea using customer research techniques. This contributes to the design of your product or service system, which you can then develop, patent, and license. Not only that, you will be able to determine the ways to finance, manufacture, and distribute your product, as well as choose the most effective methods of advertising.

At each stage you can do the work or hire it out to professionals. You may want to sell your idea to a developer or license your patent to a capable manufacturer rather than set up your own production facility. Market research and advertising can be done by an outside firm. You can also hire an accountant or lawyer to create your business plan, or you can pursue financing alternatives yourself.

This book will give you different options at each stage of your idea, from concept to finished product, giving you a hard return on your work and creativity.

Know Your Market

What makes a good idea? The only way to find out is to

know the potential market. An idea for a product or service is nothing until you know that there are customers waiting for it. Often, the degree to which you prove people will want your product determines how successful you are at getting financing, patent protection, or finding a licensor. If you don't already know the background of your idea, you will need to do some research to determine its viability.

Market research deals with gathering, processing, and analyzing information about your potential customers. This research can be used as the basis for all your development decisions, as well as for planning your advertising and budgeting. In developing your idea, you must determine what the best potential markets are, then select the means by which you can satisfy those demands.

In this way, the design of your product or service takes into account the qualities and physical characteristics that would appeal to the largest segment of your potential market. Of course, development and financing will dictate some of your decisions, as well as sheer practicality, but incorporating information gained from market research will help your idea be a success.

Marketing also covers advertising. By knowing your target market, you will be able to create effective advertising. Every business, whether it is in manufacturing or a service industry uses marketing in order to be successful.

Market Research

Before the advent of market research, producers made their products and fought it out in the marketplace to see which qualities and characteristics were preferred by the customers. That led to the concept that the best product for the best price would win the market share. Advertising was simply an attempt to notify customers about current products.

With the development of market research, businesses began attempting to identify customer needs, then developing and marketing products to satisfy those needs. The ability to accurately measure consumer behavior has been proven time and again. Using scientific polling techniques, we can determine what certain segments of society read, or watch, or buy, or believe. You can also find out consumers' attitudes, preferences, habits, and purchasing power. This research information can be used as a base for your marketing and design decisions.

Kinds of Market Research

There are different kinds of market research designed to suit the phases of development or advertising.

Market analysis and forecasting measures the market and estimates sales possibilities. You can do it yourself by gathering information on similar products or services operating in the same general area. Good forecasting relies on quantities of information, as well as the many interdependent factors of economy, competition, pricing, etc.

Performance analysis is done after you have established your business and is measured against the results of your market analysis and forecast. The performance analysis helps you evaluate how well your business is meeting its objectives in sales, share of market, sales-force performance, and costs and profits.

Product research can be anything from identifying the needs and characteristics of potential product users to testing package designs.

Advertising research determines how effective your advertising is in drawing customers. This can be done on established advertising campaigns or by testing new advertising.

Doing Your Own Market Research

Begin by studying relevant trade publications, professional magazines, and newsletters in your field. Your local library will have a periodical index listing any field you may want. When your idea has reached a certain stage of documented development, you can begin to talk to experts about the viability and value of your invention.

A good place to meet experts in the field of your idea is through trade shows, conventions, and exhibits. Find a booth or exhibit showing related products and talk to the salespeople. You'll also want to talk to editors of trade publications, representatives from service organizations, parts suppliers, and buyers and sellers. These people can help you determine all sorts of marketing specifics, including: the size of your projected market, approximate pricing, the established manufacturers of goods of that type, and how the selling is done. You can also get technical assistance in determining what are likely to be the preferred features of your product or service, what problems might be expected in production, and if anyone else is developing, producing, or currently selling anything similar.

With this assistance, you should be able to determine if your idea is viable for further development. Often, improvements are needed at this stage to better adapt your idea to current modes of production, the buying habits of your market, and the projected profit/effort ratio.

Market Researchers

If you don't want to research your potential market yourself, there are scores of researchers who have been studying the motivations of many types of consumers for decades.

Responses to various kinds of salesmanship, advertising, and other marketing techniques have already been documented by public-opinion surveys. And almost every conceivable variable affecting consumers' opinions, beliefs, suggestibility, and behavior has been investigated for every kind of group, subgroup, and culture. These large quantities of data are stored and statistically processed by computers. The procedure has been so refined that you can determine exactly what certain segments of society want in terms of your product or service.

To find a market researcher, look in your local Business-to-Business telephone directory under "Market Research and Analysis," "Marketing Consultants," "Marketing Programs and Services," and "Sales Promotion Services." Or, if you are targeting a market area larger than your local region, you can consult a major metropolitan Business-to-Business guide for nationwide companies.

Basic Procedures

There are certain general procedures in marketing research. The following are the basic steps:

1. Preliminary analysis, in which factors and variables are examined, often on the basis of a search for information on similar products or services.
2. Planning of the research study, in order to determine how the data will be obtained and organized.
3. Collection and tabulation of data, which may be primary data gathered by direct observation, experimentation, or survey, or secondary data obtained from government or expert sources.
4. Interpretation of results, arriving at conclusions and recommendations.

Surveys can be done by mail, telephone, or personal interview. The survey must be checked for validity and reliability in terms of a representative sample of the market.

Professional Evaluation

If you want further evaluation of your idea, why not get a university to do it for you? Many of the major universities in the following list charge little or nothing for providing a complete market research analysis on your idea. Simply write to these departments and get the guidelines for submitting your idea proposal.

California State University, Fresno
Bureau of Business Research and Advice
Fresno, California 93740

Carnegie-Mellon University
Center for Entrepreneurial Development
4516 Henry St.
Pittsburgh, Pennsylvania 15213

George Washington University
Innovation Information Center
2130 H St., NW
Washington, D.C. 20052

Stanford University
Innovation Center
Stanford, California 94305

University of Illinois
Bureau of Economic and Business Research
408 David Kinley Hall
Urbana, Illinois 61801

University of Utah
Utah Innovation Center
Salt Lake City, Utah 84112

Designing Your Product or Service

The design of your product or service evolves as you determine its viability in the market. Depending on the anticipated reaction of the customer, you may decide to be guided in certain ways. If research shows that most of your customers will be teenage girls and that teenage girls prefer primary colors over pastels, then you should incorporate that preference into your design.

Of course, function and practicality dictate the overall design. If your idea is a service, like a drive-through ice-cream store, then certain requirements of the system may dictate the layout of the establishment. It's a good idea to go to other drive-through businesses—whether a fast-food concern or a dry cleaner—to find out what the salespeople and customers think of that aspect of the design. You may come up with remarkable innovations based on these insights.

When you are dealing with the design of products, you also have to take into account manufacturing limitations, patent protection, and distribution requirements. If you intend to cater to industrial users, your product must fit into an existing or planned production system.

Innovation is the alteration of an existing product to better fit the market. Usually, the best ideas incorporate innovative changes in the style of the product or add desirable features. Or you can develop a new use for an established product. The current food processors are examples of blender technology expanding to include other uses.

Most invention today is done by the product research and development departments of manufacturing firms rather than by independent inventors, but a significant percentage of important ideas and products have been created by people just like you.

2 | *Protecting and Developing Your Idea*

You can legally protect your idea under any one of the three distinct fields of intellectual property law: patents, copyrights, and trademarks.

Patents are issued for innovative systems as well as for inventions. If your idea is for a new type of service system, you may want to consider patenting your process. If your idea is for a new product, it may be unique enough to qualify for patent protection. Once you have a patent, you can keep others from producing that object or using your system.

Trademarks are a symbol that is associated with a business or product. A trademark is a way to keep other people from confusing the public about the origin of their goods or service. For example, Kleenex is a trademark for paper tissues. Your idea becomes identifiable to the public by its trademark.

Copyrights protect creative material from unauthorized duplication. You can copyright material such as books, plays, music, statues, motion pictures, television programs, etc.

One thing to remember—the laws governing intellectual property are not self-inforcing. You, as owner of the copyright, trademark, or patent, must sue to receive justice if someone infringes.

Planning for Protection

When you file for a patent, the finished invention is not enough—the evolution and development of your idea must be fully documented to prove you were the originator. You are also required to describe your idea thoroughly in both words and pictures.

This means you must plan for your patent as you develop your ideas. Keep a record of everything having to do with your idea: its conception, its background, and the development and improvements as well as the setbacks. Take note of contributions made by other people, however small they might be. Document the development with sketches, photographs, and test results. Make sure to note the specific material or information that sparked innovations, as well.

Notes

Everything to do with your idea should be kept, dated, and annotated as to how it relates to your idea. Many people put their scribbles and calculations in one bound notebook, which ensures that all the material is kept together and in sequential order. If you are a note-scratcher, you will have more difficulty keeping your work organized, but there is the added benefit of shuffling certain aspects of your idea together so they can be seen at once. Either way will do, as long as the date is on each note.

If you would like protection on your idea before actually filing for a patent, give your notes on the development to someone you trust so she can read them. Then she can sign and date each page with the current date after the words "read and understood by me." Or you can get copies of your notes notarized. You can also send a copy of your notes to yourself by registered mail, leaving the envelope unopened. Any one of these measures will establish the accuracy of the dates in the evolution of your idea.

Sketches

Even if you can't draw, make sketches of your idea during development. Fine art is not the point—sketches are even better than notes for protection because they are distinctly yours. Also, your sketches will help the professional draftsman (who knows the formats and requirements of the Patent Office) when he does the official rendering of your invention.

Pictures also speak louder than words. Not only are sketches better at communicating your complex idea to another person, but they also help clarify the idea for you. You may see the need for improvements in your idea that you hadn't recognized in the abstract conception. Also, creating a sketch of your idea often helps lead you to the next stage of its development. Therefore, sketching your idea contributes to its evolution while documenting it for your patent.

Schematic diagrams show the proportions and scope of the parts of your product or system, with indications of movements during operation. Schematic drawings are used for electrical or fluid systems, or to show a sequence of operations in which one element affects another element.

Engineering drawings are similar to architectural renderings. They are cross-sectional drawings that show views from the front, the side, and the top. Dimensions, individual components, and the materials of the component parts must be noted to make the structure and operation of the product clear.

Perspective sketches are a three-dimensional rendering of your invention. Graphic computers have created a revolution in perspective sketches, and many inventors find that they help in the development of their ideas.

Prototype

Though it's not necessary to create a prototype to get a patent, it is an important step in the development process of your idea. You must be able to prove that your invention has been fully conceived in an operating form before you are granted a patent, and that's much easier when you have a working prototype to describe.

Starting with a model, you can make it as simple as paper and scotch tape. Cardboard, Bristol board, and vinyl sheets and tubes are useful materials for creating models.

When creating a working prototype, don't start from scratch. Many of the components you need may already be on the market. To research what is available, look in hardware and electronics stores, as well as checking out radio, TV, and music stores. You can also look in trade and manufacturing supply magazines, craft and hobby catalogs, the Yellow Pages, and the fourteen-volume *Thomas Register*. Use standard parts whenever possible. This will help later when you begin the production of your product for market use.

If you don't have the necessary expertise to create a prototype or a component part, don't let that stop you. You can often beg, buy, or trade for the help you need from a skilled specialist. If you need a component wired, take it to an electrician who can do it for a small charge. If the participation is substantial, you may barter with a share of the profits from the product in return for the service. This is how commercial laboratories often work. When you farm your idea out to a commercial laboratory you must supply precise drawings and design specifications. To find laboratories in your area, look in the Business-to-Business Pages under "Laboratories—Research and Development."

Don't be afraid to reveal pertinent aspects of your idea to a specialist—keeping thorough notes and evolution documentation of your idea will protect you. In addition, talking over your idea with a specialist can provide more insight than endlessly mulling it over on your own.

Testing

Whether it is a prototype created in your basement workshop or in a commercial laboratory, you learn more about your invention during testing than at any other stage. Vital improvements are often made during testing, and the results are good documentation of the development process. You may also discover additional uses for your product which you hadn't envisioned in the earlier stages of development.

In addition, a working prototype gives you credibility with investors and in the promotion of your product.

Coinventors

If a specialist or laboratory provides a solution to a major problem or is instrumental in the development of your idea, you can grant them the status of "coinventor," with rights to the invention equal to yours.

However, unless there is an agreement or assignment of the patent to one of the inventors, each inventor has the right to exploit the invention with no need to account to the other inventor(s). This is true no matter how big the percentage of ownership is on either side.

Sometimes, two or more inventors come up with the same invention around the same time. In cases like these, the Patent Office holds an *interference proceeding* which determines who was the first to create the invention. The patent is not necessarily granted to the inventor who filed first, and this is where your documentation of development (if witnessed or notarized) will verify the dates of the evolution of your idea.

3 | *Patents*

The word *patent* means open. The day a patent is granted, the schematic drawings and all the details of producing the object or working the system are made available to anyone who wants them.

This means the secrets of your innovation are made public, but you as the owner of the patent have the right "to exclude others from making, using, or selling the invention throughout the U.S." (35 U.S.C. 154). In effect, you are given a seventeen-year monopoly on your invention in return for full disclosure. At the end of that time, patent rights expire and the invention can be used or worked by anyone.

A patent is often referred to as a "license to sue" since patents grant the right to exclude others from profiting from your idea. Therefore, the value of a patent lies in the utility of the invention and the desire of others to use it or be in possession of it. If your idea is valuable, you can then either commercialize on the invention yourself or grant licenses for others to do so.

A U.S. patent is enforced through the fifty states and U.S. territories and possessions. A U.S. patent can't be enforced in Canada, Japan, Europe, or any other foreign country, but the importation of products from abroad which infringe a U.S. patent may be stopped and the infringer sued in this country.

What Is Patentable?

An invention is patentable when there is a real, potential market for a product or process that is both new and useful without being obvious. If someone else hasn't invented, published, or used it in public before, it can be patented.

Patents have been granted for products as diverse as slot machines, drive-in theaters, and computer applications. Two established products joined together in a new combination are also patentable. For example, creating a better way of putting lead into a pencil may not be patentable, but the combination of an eraser plus a lead pencil is patentable.

Sometimes an idea isn't practical to patent, such as fad items like pet rocks, or toys and dolls. In this case, a trademark for a catchy name can be much more valuable as well as easier to obtain.

What Is Unpatentable?

Many ideas aren't patentable because they aren't unique enough. If a person having ordinary skill in the art to which your idea pertains could have easily come up with your idea, then it's not usually considered patentable.

It is the product or system that is patented, not the result of the operation. Therefore, desired functions are not patentable. These include: perpetual motion machines, promotional advertising schemes, business plans, intended results of desired goals, nebulous concepts or ideas, and laws of nature.

Also, you won't be granted a patent if you have sold your product or published an article or advertisement about your idea more than one year before your filing date.

Types of Patents

There are five distinct types of patents: design, structure, process/method/system, combination-of-materials, and living-cell.

A *design* patent is a drawing of the invention, intended to protect its general appearance.

A *structure* patent is for the product itself—one unit that can be manufactured and shipped. The structure patent involves drawings and an expanded explanation of how the product works, as well as the history behind its invention, its value, examples, and alternatives for use.

Process/method/system patents use schematic diagrams to show the way a group of components work together, such as electrical wiring circuits, fluid systems, flow charts, or a sequence of processes. Usually, a system, process or service is accomplished by the invention.

Pharmaceuticals use *combination-of-materials* patents, which involve descriptions of how materials are mixed. New gene-splicing techniques are now included among the *living-cell patents*.

Filing for a Patent

You can hire a patent lawyer or patent agent to prepare the patent application, or you can prepare your own patent application. When making your decision, remember that patent law and procedure are complex, involving legal rights that can easily be lost if the patent application and the prosecution of the application are not handled properly. A patent lawyer or agent can anticipate problems regarding your application or invention that you do not have the experience to recognize.

If you decide to use a lawyer or agent, the individual must be qualified by having passed an examination given by the Patent Office. Patent agents differ from patent lawyers in that they cannot provide legal advice and assistance beyond preparing and prosecuting patent applications.

You can get a list of patent lawyers and agents registered to practice before the Patent Office by writing to:

The Superintendent of Documents
U.S. Government Printing Office
Washington, D.C. 20402

However, lawyer's charges are the major cost in obtaining your patent. The fee is usually based on the amount of time involved in preparing and in prosecuting the application, so an estimation of cost is the best you can hope for at the beginning.

If you decide to prepare your own application, the best way to learn how is to order patents on products in your field from the Patent Office. The steps involved in obtaining a patent include:

1. Preparing a disclosure of your idea
2. Conducting a patentability search on your idea
3. Preparing and filing a formal patent application in the U.S. Patent and Trademark Office
4. Prosecuting the application in the Patent Office

The average filing fee is $300, the issue fee (after you know you will get a patent and what it will say) is $500. There are also maintenance fees of $200 after four years, $400 after eight years, and $600 after twelve years.

Prior Art Search

Prior art refers to previous inventions in your field. Any product or system that is similar to yours is considered prior art. Your patent fees basically pay the Patent Office to find out if someone else has already invented, published, or used your invention in public.

However, before paying the fees of completing and filing a patent application, you can conduct a search on your own or have one made by a professional searcher. The best files and references for patent searches are kept at the U.S. Patent Office, in Crystal City, Virginia, near Washington's National

Airport. If you use a patent searcher, one in Washington, D.C. would be your best choice. If you live in a major city, you can also check your library for its collection of U.S. patents.

If your search determines that your invention is not patentable, then you are saved the cost of filing. If your search determines that your invention may be patentable, the references that were found during the search can be used as background information.

You can contact professional searchers yourself or through your patent lawyer. A brief list of professional searchers follows:

Invention Marketing, Inc.
1701 K St., NW
Washington, D.C. 20006

National Patent Trademark Co.
2208 Wisconsin Ave., NW
Washington, D.C. 20007

Government Liaison Service, Inc.
1011 Artlington Blvd.
Arlington, Virginia 22209

National Patent Search Associates
703 S 23rd St.
Arlington, Virginia 22202

Washington Patent Office Searches
1011 Arlington Blvd.
Arlington, Virginia 22209

The Patent Application

Even if you hire a patent lawyer or agent to prepare your application, you can do much of the preliminary work yourself, thereby reducing costs. You can prepare and organize your supporting material, including the written description and drawings.

The patent application involves different things for each type of patent. In both a structure patent and a process/method/system patent, you will need to write an *abstract*, a brief description of your invention and why you invented it.

The *background* of your invention includes the history of the field, prior art, related patents and their numbers, or publications. This is also the place where you explain how you got your idea and what it means to the public or the field.

The *purpose* of your invention is just that—a detailed description of its possible uses, its advantages, and its goals. You can describe as many uses as you can think of for your invention.

Starting with a brief overall *description*, you must also do a detailed description referring to numbers labeled on each component part of accompanying drawings. Dimensions can be given, as well as the description of overall operation. This must include adequate technical information so that someone skilled in the art could make the invention.

The *claims* of your invention defines that which the patent right covers and is legally the most important part of the patent application. You must list the steps involved if your invention is a system patent or the parts of the invention if it is a structure patent. If your invention qualifies, you can apply for both types of patents for the same invention; then both claims are given.

Full Disclosure

Full disclosure is required to receive a patent on your idea. However, it is possible to keep certain processes or materials secret while patenting the finished product. For example, the precise formula for Coca-Cola was never patented. But this isn't smart. Almost any secret can be broken with the right analysis by experts.

You are providing full disclosure in several parts of the patent application. In the *background,* you are supposed to give a brief history of the prior art or related subject matter involved in the conception and development of your idea. You also include alternative uses for the product, other components, and ways of operation that might be beneficial. In the *purpose,* you are supposed to explain exactly how and why your product is unique. In the *description,* you have to include specific dimensions, component parts and a step-by-step account of how the individual parts interact as a system.

Above all, don't conceal facts about the development of your invention or about relevant products that have been documented. If it is determined that you willfully concealed facts, you will not receive a patent.

Prosecution of the Patent Application

Once your application has been filed in the Patent Office, it will be assigned to an examiner with the necessary technical expertise to render an opinion. First, the examiner reviews the patent application for compliance with formal requirements; only when the application has passed does he consider the invention as it is claimed. Then the examiner researches earlier patents and publications to determine if the invention as defined by the claims is patentable over prior art.

The examiner gives his written report, called the *Examiner's Action,* to you or your patent lawyer. You have the chance to respond, reviewing the prior art the examiner located and arguing for the validity of being granted a patent. You may decide to add amendments at this time, modifying the claims of the patent application.

This may happen a couple of times before the examiner concludes the patentability of the claim. The patent can be denied or granted, or more typically, an agreement is made as to the form and scope of the claims. Failing an agreement, you can make an appeal.

Issuing the Patent

From filing to issue, the average time a patent application is kept pending is more than eighteen months. On Tuesday, the Patent Office publishes the *Official Gazette* (Government Printing Office, Dept. of Documents, Washington, D.C. 20402, 202–512–0132) abstracting all of the patents issued in a given week.

You receive the original patent document—a set of printed pages and drawings bound together with a blue ribbon and fixed under a crimson seal. Informal printed copies of the patent are published by the government and are available from the U.S. Patent and Trademark Office, which is part of the Commerce Department. The mailing address of the office is Washington, D.C. 20231.

4 | *Trademarks*

A trademark is a symbol—written or pictorial—that serves to identify a product or service as yours. Rights in patents and copyrights are based on something that was created, whereas rights in trademarks are dependent on the existence of a product or company. In a sense, it is the protection of your investment of time, money, and skill at marketing against people who want to cash in on your success.

When you register a trademark or brand name, you are granted exclusive right to use that mark or name. Whatever reputation you are able to build for the trademark belongs solely to that mark. Through advertising, you can differentiate your trademark from competing companies, to give it such appeal that a large number of consumers will prefer it to others. Once you have customer loyalty you can charge a premium price.

The Form of Trademarks

Trademark law requires the owner of a trademark to control the nature and quality of the goods or services offered under the licensed mark. Therefore, the trademark must be "dinstinctive."

This makes your trademark the most concise graphic form that denotes your business or product. It should be simple, unmistakable, applicable, and timeless. The brand name has the advantage over the trademark in that it can be read at once, whereas the meaning of the trademark must first be made known. However, the brand name has less of a visual impact.

The trademark may be a word or a device or a combination of both. It can be an invented word like "Kodak," for cameras, or something self-explanatory like "Volkswagen," which means "people's car" in German. Trademarks can also be a number of other things: letters, numerals, devices, names, the shape or rendition of the product, and combinations of colors.

Purpose of Trademarks

The primary function of a trademark is to identify the origin of the product. This is the basic difference between a patent and a trademark. The purpose of the patent is not to indicate origin but to protect a new product or a new process by which products are made or a service is accomplished.

It is debatable whether a trademark does more to protect your company from unfair competition or to protect the public from imitations. Trademark law serves to protect the interests of the manufacturer who owns the trademark; competitors who wish to prevent monopolization of symbols or expressions; and customers who don't want to be deceived or confused about goods. There is also a moral benefit to the general public: A trademark helps to avert deception in the marketplace.

The trademark also guarantees the quality of the product. In the minds of the customers, the trademark identifies goods associated with certain qualities, experiences, or characteristics. It gives assurance that goods bearing the same trademark at the next purchase will have the same characteristics.

Unfair Competition

A trademark is recognized as the exclusive property of the company which owns it. Use of the trademark by another company violates trademark law, whether or not that company intended to deceive customers. The law does not protect the material sign or mark as a creation in itself, but the use of that sign or mark in connection with a product or service.

Trademark Registration

The right in a trademark is created by use of a trademark, and common law protection is part of this right irrespective of registration. This is also where trademark law differs from patents—an inventor who hasn't patented his invention can't stop another person from making or using that product. But the owner of a trademark who has failed to register his mark may still be protected against its use by others under the condition that deception was intended.

Federal registration gives the registrant certain procedural advantages, such as a presumption of ownership, a right to sue in the federal courts, a right to claim treble damages in case of willful infringement, and in certain situations, the right to claim protection in foreign countries.

Loss of Trademark Rights

According to U.S. courts, a trademark ceases to be such when it comes to be generally understood as a generic or descriptive name of a certain type of goods. There have been spectacular cases of such loss of trademark rights involving, among others, aspirin, cellophane, shredded wheat, jello, and thermos.

Usually, a trademark is weakened and may lose its trademark status if the word is used as a noun instead of an adjective. Thermos bottle was the original demarcation, but "thermos" began to be used as a noun and thus lost its trademark status. It's best to pick a trademark name that is an adjective (descriptive or not) that is always linked to a generic noun—like Kodak camera or Kleenex tissue.

It makes no difference how such generalization takes place—if the court determines that the public sees the trademark as a description of the product or service rather than a trademark, then they deem it as such and the trademark is lost.

Also, another company can contest your right to your trademark by showing evidence of prior use.

Foreign Registration

Trademark law differs in other countries, but all have some sort of registration process. Usually, a company will test the market before registering its trademark to determine if there is sufficient business to warrant filing. Some countries won't register a trademark until it acquires distinctiveness by use.

5 | *Copyrights*

$\mathbf{A}$ copyright is the right to control or benefit from works of authorship—that is, the expressive efforts of a writer, composer, artist, or other creative individual. Copyright law mainly deals with entertainment and communications, and the intangible rights in literary, artistic, and intellectual works. As technology grows, copyright protection continues to grow as well, and now includes cable television, satellite transmissions, videocassettes, computer and communication technology.

As long as your work is original in the sense that it was created independently, it can be copyrighted even if there is a close similarity to other works in existence.

When you have a copyright, you essentially have a monopoly on the market for your creation. However, a copyright is more limited than a patent, since it doesn't prevent competition from similar works that have been created independently. For example, anyone else may write a book or play on the same subject to compete with yours. But if you have a copyright on your material, you can keep other people from reproducing it.

Purpose of Copyrights

There was a dual purpose in the development of copyright law: to protect the author in something that rightfully

27

belongs to him and to stimulate creation and promote competition by forcing others to create their own works rather than being able to freely use someone else's.

In the United States, copyright is given to original works of creation in any tangible medium of expression, including literature, music, drama, pantomime, choreography, pictures, graphics, sculpture, audiovisual works, and sound recordings. The law gives the owner of copyright the exclusive right to reproduce and distribute the copyrighted work in copies or photographs, to prepare derivative works, and to publicly perform and display the work.

However, there are certain limitations. According to the concept of *fair use*, a minor taking of copyrighted material from a work is not considered an infringement.

Your Rights

Copyrights are essentially pecuniary rights, in that they protect you against loss of income from your creation. Yet there are a set of personal rights involved as well. Since authorship is such an individual creative process, it is seen as something different from ordinary labor or investment. Some countries go so far as to provide provisions in their copyright law that give the author the "moral right" to prevent distortion of his work and to assure that he is identified as its author.

In keeping with this, throughout most of the world the duration of the copyright term is based on the life of the author. In the United States, the general term of copyright protection is the life of the author plus fifty years after the author's death. For anonymous works, pseudonymous works, and works made for hire, the term is seventy-five years from first publication or one hundred years from the date of creation of the work, whichever is shorter.

By copyright law, you are often required to affix a notice

of copyright to copies and records of published works in such a way as to give "reasonable notice" of claim of copyright. Either the symbol for copyright (©) or for records (℗), or the abbreviation "Copr." This must be written together with the year of first publication and the name of the owner of copyright. However, the omission of the notice doesn't invalidate the copyright if corrective steps are taken in a timely fashion.

How to Copyright

The simplest form of copyright is to mail yourself a copy of your material via registered mail. When you receive the letter, leave the envelope sealed. If needed in court, your unopened letter will document the date your material was completed.

6 | *Licensing*

A license is granted by the owner of a patent, trademark, or copyright. Under the terms of the license, you allow someone else to exploit or use your product or service system. In return, you are paid fees in the form of royalties or percentage of profits.

Patent Licensing

Licensing your patent is theoretically the ideal solution once you have patented your idea. It makes sense to let an experienced company with engineering, manufacturing, and sales facilities produce your product for you. Royalty payments can be made in a single lump sum, or according to the number of products sold, or in the form of percentage of income from the sale of the licensed product. The licensee also takes on your responsibility for patent enforcement and foreign rights.

However, it can be difficult to license your invention without a proven track record. Manufacturers want to know that there is a market for your idea, that it works, and how much it will cost to produce. You have to prepare the ground for licensing while you are preparing your patent application and creating a prototype of your product.

You can submit licensing proposals to companies who may be interested in your product. A licensing proposal is simply an abbreviated version of your patent application, edited to emphasize the growth potential of your product and the importance of the innovation. When you are looking for a licensee, it's best to pick a company in a field related to your product. Your product should benefit a company, not challenge products they are already producing.

There are a variety of possibilities in the rights granted by your license. It is important to have expert help in drawing up contracts and terms of payments. Though patent licensing is considered a private transaction, unregulated by the government, certain violations are considered patent misuse or antitrust violations. There are also a number of provisions that you might want to include in the contract, such as: a consulting contract, access to financial reports, exclusivity, and technical and market information.

Trademark Licensing

When you own a trademark, you can grant to another person or company the right to use your trademark. The trademark may be used in whole or in part, on an exclusive or nonexclusive basis.

In international trade, there are enterprises in various countries that seek licenses to use a trademark that has a good reputation. This is a short cut to success that saves expense in advertising and avoids promotion of a new trademark.

Manufacturers also benefit by licensing their trademarks to foreign manufacturers, thereby avoiding import restrictions, customs, taxes, and foreign exchange difficulties. By allowing a foreign company to use the trademark, the reach of the trademark is expanded.

The owner of the trademark continues to control and supervise the standards and specifications of the goods which are produced. Licensing frequently involves the sharing of technology or information which will assist in keeping the quality of the product or service high. In some countries, the law requires that the trademark license be recorded in the local Patent Office to provide public notice.

Copyright Licensing

A copyright can be split up into exclusive licenses in a variety of ways, with the grants depending on media, location, and periods of time. The licenses are granted by contracts, which are usually established within each field. Since business practices are constantly changing and growing, it is essential to hire a lawyer or agent who knows your particular field as well as contract law.

There are also certain compulsory licenses that are necessary for some types of copyright, such as phonograph records, retransmissions by cable television systems, and jukeboxes.

Licensing Agreement

Your license agreement sets out the terms and conditions under which a company is granted use of your patent. The most basic conditions are listed as follows:

1. *Agreement Title*

   Always include the date of the agreement, effective date of the agreement, your complete name, address, and telephone number; the complete name of the licensee, address, phone number, and contact name.

2. *Definitions*

   This includes the definition and description of your product or service, your patent, trademark, or copyright number.

3. *Technical Assistance*

A. Guarantee of Licensor providing all engineering, technical, manufacturing, process specifications, test data, drawings, suppliers list, etc., to the licensee.

B. Guarantee of Licensor providing all marketing information regarding the patent, including advertising and technical literature and distribution requirements.

C. Guarantee of a limited amount of direct technical assistance in the form of instruction and inspection from the Licensor (expenses to be paid by Licensee).

4. *Grant of License*

The length of term of the agreement; whether it is nontransferable, exclusive, nonexclusive, or worldwide; whether the Licensee can sublicense the patent.

5. *Compensation*

Terms of contract payment and royalty; increases; minimum royalty; sales, returns, and leases.

6. *Reports*

Guarantee that Licensee will make available for inspection sales reports, quarterly statements, computation of royalties, and books of account.

7. *Termination*

Default terms and ensuing obligations; termination on insolvency clause; right of termination and limits.

Part II
Financing Your Idea

7 | *Financing*

To start production, you need capital. If you are lucky enough to have a name and experience in your field, then there's a good chance you can get a venture capital company interested in your idea for a product or service.

But that's not the only way to raise money. There are literally billions of dollars available to individuals and businesses, in the form of grants and equity investments. Even with the investment business in a slump, there are a number of ways to get loans with extremely flexible terms—such as extended repayment periods, low interest rates, and cosigner guarantees.

The more money you have to fund your venture, whether it's a start-up business or a special project, the more likely you are to succeed. It helps that financing tends to build on itself. Once you have commitments for certain sums of money, it becomes easier to get more.

There are many financing options: "free money" from foundation grants, straight debt (loan), or selling public or private equity in your business or venture (your profits pay the dividends). You can also chose a combination of financing—be it SBA loan and private debt, or a foundation grant and bank loan.

Loans

Loans are "straight debt" financing, which means they

must be paid back, with interest, at specified times. If you want to finance your venture with loans, then you will need to decide on public or private debt, short- or long-term payment. Banks, insurance companies, and private individuals are good loan sources.

Most lending institutions, whether they are private or federal—such as the Small Business Administration or federal agencies—expect you to provide collateral or a cosigner.

Collateral

Collateral is any property or valuable asset which can be offered as security for your loan. If you are unable to repay your loan, the lender sells your collateral and receives the money in lieu of repayment. Lenders prefer easily liquidated assets as collateral, such as automobiles, boats, stocks, bonds, insurance policies, property, or home.

If you already have an established business, many institutions will lend against bills, accounts or notes that are due from others, but not against inventory. Business collateral can also include: business equipment, property, bills of lading, warehouse receipts for goods in storage, and contracts.

Don't put up all your collateral for a single loan. Conserve your collateral, because once you pledge an item against a loan, you can't use it on another loan application.

Cosigners

Having a cosigner makes getting a loan much easier. Lenders like it when someone is willing to put her name and money on the line for you, in case you can't make the payments. Keep in mind that lenders won't examine your cosigner's earnings and dependability as carefully as they do yours.

You can't use your spouse as a cosigner; in fact, most

banks ask that your spouse also sign your personal loan. You will have to turn to other family members or friends to find your cosigner.

Selling Equity

When you sell equity, what you are doing is selling stock in your venture, whether it is done privately or publicly. The investor receives payment on his investment depending on the success of your venture and its growth.

There are hundreds of firms whose sole business is to provide financing for new and growing businesses. There are also individual investors, known as a venture capitalists, who supply private investment in the form of a loan as well as taking equity in your venture.

You can't sell equity publicly until your business is established and has books on which to base its financial stability. Public offerings will be discussed later, under "Expansion."

Grants

There are certain requirements you must fulfill to qualify for a foundation or government grant. Your idea must be involved in an area of humanitarian interest, such as culture, education, health-related or social service. Even if your business is intended to be profit making, you might qualify for full funding by a private foundation.

A grant proposal is less complicated than a professional business plan, and can be considered the first step in the development of your business plan for next approaching private investors.

8 | *Loans*

Loans, either alone or in combination with other forms of financing, are most typically the way capital for a new venture is raised. When you are applying for a loan, whether it's from a bank, a lending institution, or a friend or relative, you need to research your proposed venture in a way that will satisfy the lender's concerns. The preparation you do will determine the results.

Personal Loans

Personal loans from a financial institution are the fastest, easiest loans to get. Interest may be higher than with a typical business loan, but this "seed" capital can mean the difference between obtaining a business loan or being turned down. Besides, the interest is deductible on your income-tax return.

Many personal loans don't even require collateral. If you have established a good relationship with your bank, you could get a loan simply on your signature. The usual qualifying standards are: employment by the same organization for at least a year; the same address for at least six months; and a previous credit history from purchasing your car or property.

Banks don't grant personal loans to start a business, but there are other reasons you can give for wanting a personal loan, including: auto or home repairs, vacation, educational expenses, medical or dental work, emergency expenses, home improvement, etc. The bank doesn't require proof of what you need the loan for and would rather you use the money for something useful instead of paying it off early after cancelling the vacation you planned.

In addition, you can apply for more than one loan from more than one banking institution. Fill out the applications and apply for them all on the same day; that way you can honestly answer that you don't have other loans outstanding at the time of application.

Banks also offer personal credit under various names, such as ready reserve, checking account backup, executive credit plans, etc. You can usually apply for these types of personal credit on the basis of having maintained an account with your bank for a certain period of time. This can bring you up to thousands of dollars with just a signature.

Business Loans

To get a business loan, you must have an established business. This means at the very least you need a name, address, phone number, stationery, and business cards. It helps if you have a comprehensive business plan and can talk the language of the lending officer in terms of profit and loss, overhead, fixed expenses, etc. If you can't do that, it might be worth your while to find a business partner who can help you with the financial end of your venture.

You need to be prepared with the information that lenders are looking for; this is usually organized in the form of a business plan. Lenders will want to know:

1. What is the actual or potential profit of the venture?
2. What is the actual expense of the venture?

3. What is the ratio of fixed expenses (property, rent, equipment) to variable expenses (materials, production labor, etc.)
4. How many people will be employed?
5. What will the borrowed money be used for?
6. What are the repayment terms you are seeking?

Types of Loans

There are various types of business loans, including: inventory loans, working capital loans, equipment loans, property investment loans, accounts receivable loans, mortgage loans, disaster loans, etc. Terms vary for each of these.

Short-term loans usually have repayment periods under a year—30, 60, 90, 120 days, etc. There is also the option of renewing the loan term for another 60 days. As long as you pay part of the loan, banks will usually agree if you pay the interest in advance.

If your business is a corporation, then *commercial paper* may be a good source of short-term money. Commercial paper is a promissory note sold by corporations to individuals or other corporations. These notes are unsecured, which means you don't need collateral. You also don't pay monthly payments—the entire amount is due at the end of the loan period.

Compensating balance loans are made if you already have money in an account; then your business can borrow against that money. Banks will lend you up to five times what you have in your account, as long as you sign a pledge not to touch the balance. These types of loans are made quickly—usually within 24 to 48 hours after you apply.

Revolving credit is when a bank sets aside a certain amount of money as a credit to your business against which you can write checks. Revolving credit differs from a loan in that the money stays in the possession of the bank until you write the check. There is usually a charge for setting up and maintaining your revolving credit, as well as interest on the money you have borrowed.

Some commercial banks have developed *two-tier lending* which is a borrowing rate below the prime rate for small businesses. For a list of banks that offer two-tier lending rates, write to:

Chief Counsel for Advocacy
Small Business Administration
1441 L Street NW
Washington, D.C. 20005

Private Financing

There are a number of private finance companies, banks, and insurance companies that will either lend you money or help you obtain financing from other sources.

There are many *foreign-owned banks* interested in investing in American businesses. These banks are not bound to obey U.S. banking regulations, which allows them a certain flexibility in terms. Two of the larger foreign-owned banks are Britain's Barclay Bank and the Bank of Montreal, but you can consult your Yellow Pages for a foreign bank near you.

Finance Companies specialize in ongoing financing to small businesses. Since finance companies are actively involved in your venture, they tend to give advice on running your business, as well. The cost may be higher than a simple bank loan, but the security of having additional capital if you need it may offset the difference.

Life Insurance Companies are state regulated and are limited in the type of investments they can make. They specialize in medium- to long-term credit, and often take stock warrants (options) in a company in exchange for financing.

If you are having difficulty getting a lender to finance your business, *T.H.E. Insurance Company* issues an insurance policy to protect lenders against bankruptcy. With this insurance policy, private institutions are often more willing to give you capital. You can write to T.H.E. Company for more information at:

T.H.E. Insurance Company
180 Bent Street
Cambridge, Massachusetts 02141
(617) 494-5300

Federal, State, and Local Loans

Many states, counties, and towns offer long-term low-interest business loans to people who are starting new businesses or expanding an established business that will bring jobs into the area. Typical areas of lending are real estate, construction, and business equipment financing.

Contact your State Development Commission for more information on state and local loans. Once your state has granted you a loan, it may be easier to get local financing for your venture.

Many federal government agencies, departments, and administrations also lend money to businesses. Most of these agencies can be located by calling the D.C. area:

Agency for International Development
Community Services Administration
Housing and Urban Development
Federal Reserve System
Health, Education and Welfare Agency
Maritime Administration
Office of Trade Adjustment
Public Housing Administration
Treasury Department of the U.S.
Urban Renewal Administration

Farmers Home Loan

The Farmers Home Loan (FmHa) is the loan program of the Farmers Home Administration, offering guaranteed loans to growing businesses. FmHa loans have ranged from $7,000 to $33 million, with the average around $900,000.

The FmHa loan gives preference to distressed areas and rural communities of less than 25,000 inhabitants. It will loan money for any worthwhile business purpose. If your business creates jobs, then your loan has a greater chance of approval.

The minimum equity requirement up front is 10 percent, and the interest rate of the loans are about the same as private lending institutions. The loans are fairly long term: 30 years for construction, 15 years for equipment, and 7 years for working capital.

There are over 1,800 county offices of Farmers Home Administration, so there is probably one in your area. Or you can write to:

Farmers Home Administration
United States Department of Agriculture
Washington, D.C. 20250

Economic Development Administration Funds

If you try and are unable to borrow from outside sources, you can apply for a loan under the Economic Development Administration. Two-thirds of all counties in the U.S. have been designated as "economically depressed," and if your business is located in one of these counties, you qualify for funds.

However, you must put up at least 15 percent of the financing and get 5 percent of the financing needed from a state or a nongovernmental community organization, such as Community Development Corporation.

For a list of economically depressed areas, the application form and other information, write to any of EDA's six regional offices, or:

Office of Business Development
Economic Development Administration, Room 7876
14th/Constitution Avenue NW
Washington, D.C. 20230
(202) 377-2000

9 | *The Small Business Administration*

The Small Business Administration is an independent federal agency that assists, counsels, and protects American small businesses. The SBA provides financial assistance as well as management training.

The SBA makes a limited number of direct loans to small businesses. There are two requirements of an SBA loan: You must have been turned down for a loan by a commercial lender and you must have collateral. Businesses dealing with real estate, publishing, or investment are not eligible for SBA loans.

However, most often, the SBA cosigns bank loans for small businesses after they are unable to attain financing on their own. Because these businesses aren't bankable without the SBA guarantee, they are usually considered medium- to high-risk ventures. You or your company may lack capital, have insufficient collateral, or have a minimum track record in the field and still get an SBA cosignature.

As a public service organization, the Small Business Administration sets limits on interest rates that banks can charge you on a loan it guarantees. Normally, this is several points below comparable bank loans. You apply for an SBA loan guarantee at your bank.

Reasons the SBA Will Reject You

There are certain types of ventures that the SBA won't get involved in, including:

1. Professional gambling
2. Businesses obtaining more than half their sales from alcoholic beverages
3. Newspapers, magazines, radio, or TV
4. Recreational facilities, *unless* they benefit the general public
5. Lending or investment firms (see *SBIC* at the end of this chapter)
6. Speculative real estate
7. Businesses that can get funds elsewhere

Loan Programs

The SBA has three programs through which direct loans or guaranteed bank loans are made: the 7A Term Loan, the Economic Opportunity Loan (EOL), and the Operation Business Mainstream (OBM) Loan.

The SBA also makes line-of-credit guarantees for up to $350,000. The line is secured by specific contracts for your business's product or service, and the funds may only be used to pay for materials and labor on the assigned contracts. Lines of credit typically run for a year.

Certified Lending Institutions

The final decision for granting an SBA-guaranteed loan is made by financial institutions designated "certified lending institutions." You can cut the processing time if you apply for your loan at a certified lending institution.

Control Data Corporation, authorized by the SBA to provide guaranteed loans, has Business Centers around the country. These Business Centers offer data processing services, business planning, marketing assistance, and lending services. For more information, contact your local Control Data Business Center or the main office at:

Control Data Corporation
5241 Viking Drive
Bloomington, Minnsota 55435
(612) 893-4200

The Money Store Investment Corporation offers SBA-guaranteed loans in branch locations in twelve states. For more information, contact the Union headquarters of The Money Store at (908) 686–2000.

Allied Lending Corporation provides SBA-guaranteed loans for the Washington, D.C. area:

Allied Capital Lending Corporation
1666 K Street NW
Washington, D.C. 20006
(202) 331-1112

Fortistar Corporation provides SBA-guaranteed loans for New York State:

Fortistar Corporation
115 East 57th Street
New York, N.Y. 10022
(212) 644-0920

The First Commercial Bank provides SBA-guaranteed loans in Los Angeles:

The First Commercial Bank
Los Angeles, California 92071
(213) 362-0200

Small Business Investment Corporations

Small Business Investment Corporations are licensed and regulated by the SBA to supply venture capital and long-term financing to small businesses. There are about three hundred SBICs in the country, and most are affiliated with banks.

The limit the SBIC can invest in a business is up to $100,000, and the lengthy application process takes more time than with private institutions. For more information, call or write:

SBA (or SBIC Division)
1441 L Street NW
Washington, D.C. 20005

The Minority Enterprise Small Business Investment Company (MESBIC) is another type of SBIC which provides financing and assistance to minority-owned businesses or economically disadvantaged persons. For more information, call or write:

American Association of MESBICs
13th Floor, 1413 K Street, NW
Washington, D.C. 20005
(202) 347-8600

10 | *Equity Financing*

The term "venture capital" refers to an investment of funds, usually in newer businesses, with an expectation of continuing returns on the profits. This is how equity differs from loans, which are paid off plus interest. Private investment is not regulated by the SEC if fewer than thirty-five investors agree to hold stocks in your business for more than two years.

Different types of people invest in new businesses: professionals, such as venture capitalists and "angels"; institutional investors; nonprofessional investors, such as doctors and lawyers; and friends and relatives. Nonprofessionals may want to invest with high expectations of quick profit. Many nonprofessional investors choose to provide advice as well.

There are about a thousand venture capital firms in the United States. More than half are also SBICs, Small Business Investment Companies regulated by the Small Business Administration.

Types of Investment

Most venture capital firms prefer *interest-bearing debt* rather than a straight equity deal. This way, they are assured of receiving an annual income on their investment. Secured debt is backed by an asset that is pledged to guarantee the payment of the debt. A house mortgage is a good example of secured debt. Any debt without an asset pledged as collateral is considered unsecured debt.

Common or capital stock is a certificate of ownership of equity in the company. Preferred stock has advantages over common stock, such as guaranteed dividends or prior rights in a liquidation.

Debt with warrants is a type of loan, in that your company is obligated to repay a certain amount of money over a period of time at an agreed-upon rate. Warrants are the right to buy shares of common stock at a fixed price sometime in the future.

Convertible debentures are a type of loan, with the option of turning the remaining debt into stock.

Business Plan

A business plan is the objective assessment of your business and your goals. An investor will usually skim your business plan, so clarity and brevity are essential. Yet, venture capitalists use the information in your business plan to determine if they will invest in your company, so you must make all the pertinent information available.

It's best if you can adjust the business plan slightly to appeal to each potential investor. Venture capitalists inevitably have preferred areas of investment, and you can emphasize aspects of your company that might be of particular interest to them.

Venture capitalists are also intrigued by anything that is unique about your product or service. Any patents, trademarks, unusual technology, production method, or increase in quality of a service or product will help sell your proposal.

The professional experience of your company's founders and managers, including where they have worked and how well they have performed in the past, are also important.

Investors look for experience in the marketing, finance, and production sides of your business.

You must make the terms of the investment deal very clear and include the latest balance sheet (if it is an established business). Emphasize the growth potential of your business to show there will be a big return on investment.

Lastly, venture capitalists are usually interested in the future salability of your company. Their business is to invest in companies, then become liquid so they can invest again. Give them a list of the larger, publicly traded companies in the same industry. It will be easier for you to raise money if another company has already pioneered in your field successfully.

Delivering Your Business Plan

Theoretically, you could submit your plan to dozens of venture capitalists, but this may undermine your chances of raising funds rather than improve them. The SEC prefers businesses to send their business plan to fewer than thirty-five investors. Federal regulations limit you to a hundred potential investors, but certain states have set the limit at twenty. It's worth your while to investigate, select, and approach the venture capitalists before sending them your business plan.

The best way to deliver a plan is through a third party. The third party is, in effect, recommending you to the investor, prompting the investor to read the plan with more serious attention. You can use almost anyone whose liaison with the investor is positive: accountants, lawyers, consultants, bankers, and other entrepreneurs.

Sample of a Business Plan

The purpose of a business plan is to raise capital from one or more private investors. You don't need to register your plan with the SEC since it is a private transaction.

You can write your business plan yourself, but it's likely you will need some assistance from a lawyer in the financial terms of the offering. You may also want to hire the services of an accountant for projections. Or you can use the *Pink Sheets*, a compellation of stocks and share prices of small companies published by the SEC. This way you can keep abreast of companies similar to yours that are making public offerings and use their projections as a basis for your own.

Typically included in the plan are:

1. *The History of Company or Field*

   Briefly summarize your proposed business endeavor, using examples of successful companies in your field.

2. *Business Summary*

   a. Principal products or services, including the brand names, price ranges, and quality.
   b. Describe the unique features of the business and products. Compare these objectively with the competition.
   c. Give specific goals on annual sales growth and profits, using as support material the financial statements of competition in your field.
   d. Describe patents or trademarks and other trade advantages, such as geographical location or labor incentives.
   e. Describe any trends in the business market or economy that may affect your company.

3. *Production and Personnel Plan*

   a. Brief description of production process
   b. Special skills needed in production
   c. Number of employees needed and their positions

d. Percentage of labor content in cost of goods

4. *Products or Service*

a. Principal vendors and suppliers
b. Description of materials and supplies, including storage requirements
c. Inventory
d. Distribution

5. *Marketing and Sales*

a. Describe the market. History, size, trend, and your product's position in the market, identifying established companies used as source material.
b. Make forward and backward projections of the market—is it growing or stable or in decline?
c. Identify your market (define your customers by age, sex, geography, minority group status, or income).
d. Tell how the product will be sold.
e. Supply advertising annual budget and projected media.

6. *Competition*

a. List major competition, location, sales earnings, percent of market, and strengths and weaknesses.
b. Indicate whether new competition is entering the field.
c. Compare your prices and production with the competition.
d. Determine your share of the market.

7. *Management*

a. Resumes of management
b. Analysis of reputation, capabilities, and attitude
c. Credit checks and personal financial statements of management

    d. Proposed salary and compensation for each
        member of management and/or owners, with
        salary increases

8. *Financial Reports*
    a. Projected profit-and-loss statement (for 90 days
        and three years)
        1) Sales
        2) Cost of goods
        3) Overhead, fixed and variable
        4) Selling expenses
        5) Taxes
    b. Earnings projected (for one year)
    c. Accounting principles for depreciation, taxes,
        inventories, etc.
    d. Any lawsuits or bankruptcies
    e. Principal bank
    f. What you will use the investment for (working
       capital, equipment, land, etc.)

9. *Enclosures*

An important part of your business plan is the
enclosures, which can catch an investor's eye and
favorably affect the consideration of your proposal.
Enclosures include:
a) product literature
b) graphs
c) unusual exhibits
d) samples
e) letters of recommendation
f) letters of intent

Financial Terms

A complete business plan includes the financial terms of
investment. The financial terms include: the percentage of

the company being sold, the total price for this percentage, the minimum investment sought, and the value of the company.

If you have an established business, you must include an audited financial statement from a reputable accounting firm. A company-generated statement is not given much credence since investors want the accuracy confirmed.

The following terms must be negotiated with your investors:

1. Seats on the Board of Directors, frequency of financial statements, and right of inspection of books
2. Registration rights and timetables for selling the investor's stock or buying new stock first if the company goes public
3. Working capital established, net worth of the company, and restrictions on dividends to keep the business from being drained of money
4. Insurance issues settled: property and product liability insurance, and key-man life insurance
5. Employment contracts with key personnel, specifying salary and bonus terms

Merrill Lynch puts out a free, 24-page booklet, *Understanding Financial Statements*. With this book, you will learn how to read and understand a balance sheet, cash flow statement, and profit-and-loss statement. Any local Merrill Lynch office will send you a copy, or write to the general office:

Merrill Lynch Pierce Fenner & Smith Inc.
World Financial Center North Tower
New York, New York 10281
(212) 637-7455

or:

Merrill Lynch
1185 Avenue of the Americas
New York, New York 10016
(212) 328-8500

The Small Business Administration has several pamphlets on writing business plans: *Small Marketeer Aid #153; Business Plan for the Small Service Firm; Small Marketeer Aid #150; Business Plan for Retailer; Management Aid for Small Manufacturers #218; Business Plan for Manufacturers.*

Small Business Administration (SBA)
P.O. Box 15434
Fort Worth, Texas 76119
(800) 368-5855

Venture Capital Resource Publications

The Capital Publishing Company is the clearinghouse for most industrywide information on venture capital. It offers several publications, including a monthly newsletter entitled *Venture Capital Journal.*

The Guide to Venture Capital Sources, 9th ed., is an informative guide that has articles by venture capitalists focusing on all phases of funding. Its most useful feature is a geographically indexed directory with project, field, and geographical preferences included.

For more information write or call:

Capital Publishing Corporation
2 Laurel Avenue
P.O. Box 348
Wellesley Hills, Massachusetts 02181
(617) 235-5405

The National Venture Capital Association offers its membership directory free on request:

National Venture Capital Association
1730 North Lynn St., Suite 400
Arlington, Virginia 22209
(703) 528-4370

The National Association of Small Business Investment
Companies (NASBIC) offers a twice-monthly newsletter
from Washington, D.C., which includes up-to-date
information on the venture capital industry. The NASBIC
membership directory can be purchased for $1 by writing
to:

National Association of Small Business Investment
Companies
618 Washington Building
Washington, D.C. 20005
(202) 638-3411

A good reference for more than a thousand venture capital
sources is *A Handbook of Business Finance and Capital
Sources*. It contains information on financing techniques
and instruments for both private and government sources of
capital. Call or write:

Dileep Rao, PhD.
InterFinance Corporation
305 Foshay Tower
Minneapolis, Minnesota 55402
(612) 338-8185

11 | *Grants*

Foundation grants are a rich source of funding that many people neglect to explore. Individuals, entrepreneurs, initiators of projects, and businesses can apply for grants. You can apply for as many grant and awards as you qualify for.

The most typical areas to find funding for your business are: foundation program-related investments, "flow-through" funding from nonprofit organizations, and federal research and development awards.

Foundation Program-related Investment

Nonprofit organizations will invest in your business even if it is run for profit. This form of investment is known as a program-related grant and is made to any business, organization, or individual who furthers the charitable aims of the foundation. To qualify, your business must meet the foundation's definition of "socially beneficial."

Lists of private foundations can be found in your local library, along with their qualifications and the average award amounts granted. All you have to do is write to the foundation for guidelines to find out if your business qualifies, then send in your application and grant proposal (an abbreviated form of a business plan).

The following are general reference sources which contain information on thousands more foundations:

The Foundation Center is an information clearinghouse that maintains national libraries in Chicago, New York City, and Washington, D.C., as well as regional libraries in almost every state.

The *Foundation Directory* lists 2,800 foundations. The directory lists the foundation's name and address, purpose and activities, and the number and dollar amounts of grants awarded each year. You can find this directory in any Public Library.

The *Foundation Grants Index* lists grants of more than $5,000 made by the three-hundred major foundations. It lists the names of the recipients, the purposes of the grants, and the dollar amounts awarded. This compilation can also be found in any large library. *The Catalog of Federal Domestic Assistance* and the *Annual Register of Grant Support* list programs, procedures for requesting applications, names of agency officials, and awards given each year.

Profit Working With Nonprofit

Government agencies usually award grants to nonprofit organizations, such as colleges, community organizations, or clubs. But these organizations often subcontract businesses for certain aspects of their projects. If your idea can be successfully linked to a nonprofit organization, your business could receive the money through the nonprofit agency.

Another alternative is for an individual or business to use the tax-exempt status of an established nonprofit corporation as a "flow-through." It's best to locate a nonprofit organization whose purpose and activites are compatible with yours, then work directly with the executives of the organization in proving your venture serves their goal.

In "flow-through" financing, the money is paid directly to the nonprofit organization, which in turns pays you. The established nonprofit organization is usually given 3 to 7 percent of the funding raised as a flow-through fee. There is no upfront fee paid to the sponsor or parent nonprofit organization.

To find a nonprofit organization that will be willing to sponsor you, check the directory of local nonprofit organizations available in your community library. Local health and welfare planning groups, as well as the community, city, and state-run bureaus can point you to nonprofit organizations that would be interested in your service or product. In addition, don't neglect the nationwide nonprofit organizations which have outlets in your area—such as United Way, Salvation Army, etc. A reference book that contains a list of national organizations is the *Encyclopedia of Associations*, by Gale Research.

Research and Development Awards

The 1982 Small Business Innovation Research Act ensures that small businesses receive a percentage of research-and-development awards made by federal agencies. Each participating federal agency makes awards to small businesses on a competitive basis.

If a federal agency has a research-and-development budget over $100 million, it must devote a percentage of its research funds to establish Small Business Innovation Research programs. The SBIR has funded more than three-thousand businesses. Nearly half of the awards have been to firms with fewer than ten employees.

For more information, call or write to the following agencies for their guidelines:

Department of Agriculture
Office of Grants and Program Systems
Department of Agriculture
1300 Rosslyn Commonwealth Building, Suite 103

Arlington, Virginia 22209
(703) 235-2628

Department of Defense
Director, Small Business and Economic Utilization
Office of Secretary of Defense, Room 2A340, Pentagon
Washington, D.C. 20301
(202) 697-9383

Department of Education
SBIR Program Coordinator
Office of Educational Research and Improvement
Department of Education, Mail Stop 40
Washington, D.C. 20208

Department of Energy
SBIR Program Manager
U.S. Department of Energy
Washington, D.C. 20545

Department of Health and Human Services
Director, Office of Small and Disadvantaged Business
Utilization
Department of Health and Human Services
200 Independence Avenue, SW, Room 513D
Washington, D.C. 20201

Department of Interior
Chief Scientist
Bureau of Mines
U.S. Department of the Interior
2401 E Street NW
Washington, D.C. 20241

Department of Transportation
Director, Transportation System Center
Department of Transportation
Kendall Square
Cambridge, Massachusetts 02142

Environmental Protection Agency
Office of Research Grants and Centers
(RD 675)
Office of Research and Development
Environmental Protection Agency
401 M Street SW
Washington, D.C. 20460

National Aeronautics and Space Administration
SBIR Office
Code R
National Aeronautics and Space Administration
600 Independence Avenue SW
Washington, D.C. 20546

National Science Foundation
SBIR Program Manager
National Science Foundation
1800 G Street NW
Washington, D.C. 20550

Nuclear Regulatory Commission
Director, Administration and Resource Staff
Office of Nuclear Regulatory Research
Nuclear Regulation Commission
Washington, D.C. 20460

Creating a Grant Proposal

Your grant proposal is a representation of your business—make it clear and professional. Be sure to make a copy of each application before sending it in. You may need to refer to a specific part when you follow up.

1. *Title Page*

Always include a title page, with your complete name, address, and telephone number; current date; the complete name of the foundation, address, phone number and contact name; and the name of the grant you are applying for.

2. *Proposal*

In your proposal, you should describe your project or business clearly and completely. Don't beat around the bush—sell the foundation on your venture. Make the language optimistic, emphasizing the potential for growth in your particular field and the way in which your venture will contribute to the foundation's goals. Make sure you specifically address:

• What you intend to accomplish if you are funded. What exactly is the product, service, project, or activity?

• Who will support your business or who will you serve? Specifically define your customers by age, sex, geography, minority group status, or income.

• Production methods (the practical considerations of achieving your goals).

• What you will specifically use the funding for (working capital, equipment, land, etc.).

3. *Attachments*

Each foundation will require different support materials. However, the following is a typical list of information you will need to have on hand:

A. *Individual:*
   1. Degrees and awards
   2. Resume of professional experience
   3. Portfolio (artwork, project summaries, etc.)

B. *Start-up Business:*
   1. Projected profit and loss statements (for ninety days and three years)
   2. Earnings projection (for one year)
   3. Resumes of management personnel

       4. Personal IRS returns (past three years)
       5. Any lawsuits or bankruptcies
  C. *Established Business:*
       1. Balance sheets
       2. Accounts receivables
       3. Profit-and-loss statements (for ninety days and three years)
       4. Earnings projection (for one year)
       5. Business and personal IRS returns (past three years)
       6. Machinery or equipment owned (value)
       7. Any lawsuits or bankruptcies
  D. *Nonprofit Organization or Project Sponsored by Nonprofit*
       1. Budgets (last year, current year, and projected)
       2. Past and present funding support (government, corporate, and foundation)
       3. A Board of Directors list
       4. A copy of the nonprofit organization's 501 (C)(3) IRS letter that documents tax-exempt status.

References

The references you include in your grant proposal can be chosen for name recognition or standing in the field, but it helps if your references are enthusiastic about your venture and understand your goals. It may be your only chance to actively "sell" your proposal to the foundation or nonprofit organization.

Part III
Producing and Manufacturing Your Idea

12 | *Production and Manufacturing through a Contractor*

Depending on your success at obtaining financing, you can either produce and distribute your product entirely on your own or contract out all or part of the development and manufacturing. Unlike a licensee who pays you to use your patent, you have to pay a developer and cover the costs.

There are various reasons for contracting portions of the production. Development covers a broad range of activities, and the time you could be spending in marketing is lost in management, production design, testing, and dealing with suppliers. If you don't have the skill, facilities, or time to develop the product yourself, or the expertise needed is too specialized and costly, then contract it out. Or if the market for your idea is too small for you to profit in the production, then you can piggyback on another manufacturer's product line.

When you work with developers, you need to be able to convey your invention as clearly and thoroughly as possible. Any preliminary work you do will also cut down costs. It's essential to deal with a developer already experienced in your field, but don't worry that someone will steal your idea. Confidentiality is assured by the development contract.

Product developers are primarily concerned with getting the invention to function as it should, by working with the inventor. The *industrial designer* is concerned with overall function, structure, and performance, with an eye to marketability. Usually, the designer then supervises the *general contractor*, who creates the working prototype for manufacture. A *manufacturing company* may or may not do the actual factory work, but it is responsible for the finished product. *Subcontractors* can be hired by the manufacturing company to manufacture the subsystems or assemble the product.

Product Development Companies

Look in your local Yellow Pages to get names of product development companies and check their reputation with the Better Business Bureau. The following are a few well-established companies that deal with development:

Design & Development Models
1070 West King's Highway
Coatsville, Pennsylvania 19320
(215) 384-0474
Models, mechanical prototypes

Model Builders, Inc.
6155 S. Oak Park Ave.
Chicago, Illinois 60638
(312) 586-6500
Models, research and development

Precision Forms, Inc.
107 Route 23
Riverdale, New Jersey 07457
Research and development, design, machine shop

Production Previews, Inc.
29 E 21st St.
New York, New York 10010
(212) 982-2290
Mechanical prototypes, research and development

Sail Engineering
P.O. Box 17036
Richmond, Virginia 23226
(804) 288-4819
Models, prototypes, production processes

Scale Models Unlimited
111 Independence Dr.
Menlo Park, California 94025
(414) 324-2515
Models, prototypes, technical

Invention Promoters

Don't confuse developers with invention promoters, otherwise known as idea brokers, invention developers, technology or marketing consultants. These organizations make promises that range from developing your invention, to preparing and filing a patent application, to finding you a licensee. You will usually find them advertised on TV or in magazines and newspapers, offering free information to inventors.

There has been a lot of outspoken denunciation of these invention promoters who try to get inventors to pay a high fee for an ill-prepared patent application and market analysis that is comprised only of general statistics. So be careful.

Selling Your Patent

If you don't want to spend the time and effort licensing your patent, and you don't want to coordinate the development and manufacturing of the product yourself, the third alternative is to sell your patent outright. The risk is that if your product catches on, you can lose substantial income over a period of time. However, by selling you receive one lump sum up front and avoid the risks involved in a product's failing or being a transitional or fad item.

13 | *Production and Manufacturing On Your Own*

The development of your idea involves designing, testing, changing, then redesigning it until a practical, functional product is created. This production process consists of both analysis and synthesis—analysis of how something might better work or be produced, and synthesis of the fortuitous and necessary conditions imposed by standardized production methods.

This is why developing your own product with the help of a few specialists can pay off in the long run. Since it is your creation, you are often the best person to help solve these problems in a way that enhances your product. You will find exactly where the problems are in the product itself and in the production methods.

However, there are many things to consider before taking on production responsibilities of your own. Not only must you supervise the manufacturing facility and its employees, keeping the flow of materials going from suppliers to final destination, but there are also financial and legal considerations in the office overhead, insurance, salaries, and benefits to think about.

If you can, buy an existing business that is similar to yours. That's a good way to get the machinery and materials you need for production without expending the time and effort needed to create a manufacturing facility from scratch. To find businesses for sale, look in the classified ads under "Business Opportunities."

The Development Process

The key to development is planning. Planning usually starts in the design phase; you need to use materials that are easy and cheap to obtain and design standardized components so the product can be efficiently assembled.

You have to know the tolerances of your materials and how to work within those tolerances. You also have to determine the correct sequence for component assembly and product assembly.

Machinery

There is a substantial capital investment necessary to tool automatic machinery and processes. Often this capital must be committed long before production begins and before a true market for the product has been established. This means a high risk for investors.

Whenever possible, buy used machinery when you are starting out. Dealers and auctions are good sources. The difference in price could mean the difference in getting your manufacturing facility running and bogging down in bills. Ideally, you want each machine to pay for itself within three years.

Used office equipment may also be purchased. This includes everything from copy machines to computers.

Suppliers

There are thousands of suppliers of all kinds of materials and standardized components. It's important to find suppliers who will give you plenty of time to pay for your materials (thirty days is better than fifteen or COD). Take time to phone different suppliers and compare pricing and billing.

In addition, many suppliers can provide important information in your field, such as the current trend in pricing and customer preferences. You can talk to the supply representatives and find out if they had heard of your kind of product before, as well as sound them out for any advice they might have on using their material or components. They may have ideas for a better way to create the finished product with their material.

To find suppliers in your area, you can consult the *Thomas Register*, a reference book found in your local library, directories from trade magazines and catalogs, and your Business-to-Business telephone directory.

If you have to do a lot of buying from different suppliers, it might be a good idea to hire a purchasing agent. Your agent can track down the suppliers who will provide the best prices for the quantity of material you want. You can locate a purchasing agent in the Business-to-Business directory or hire one through an employment agency.

Certifications and Approvals

Inspections and rating classifications are designed to protect the public and products already in existence. Like building codes, each state and region has its own approval and certification processes in the areas of health, energy, and fire safety. Some cities, like New York and Los Angeles, have relatively difficult approval processes, and it may be worth your time and effort to launch your product elsewhere.

If you have to provide results of testing on your product, there are many laboratories that do such testing. The American Society of Mechanical Engineers and the American Society for Testing and Materials in Philadelphia both issue testing standards. The National Bureau of Standards in Washington, D.C. has publications on almost everything pertaining to testing and measurements. The National Technical Information Service offers current publications on testing in many different fields.

Thomas Publishing Company
1 Penn Plaza
New York, New York 10001

Thomas Register of American Manufacturers, Thomas Register Catalog File, Thomas Regional Directory are published by Thomas Publishing Company.

American Society for Testing and Materials
1916 Race St.
Philadelphia, Pennsylvania 19103

American Society of Heating, Refrigerating and Air Conditioning
1791 Tullie Circle, NE
Atlanta, Georgia 30329

American Society of Mechanical Engineers
345 E 47th St.
New York, New York 10017

National Technical Information Service
5285 Port Royal Rd.
Springfield, Virginia 22161
(703) 487-4640

Mass Production

Mass production begins with the design of the product. Component parts must be adaptable to production and assembly. The entire production process from the flow of raw material to packaging is coordinated and planned. In fact, every element of bringing the product to market must be an integral part of the production plan, including advertising, market research, and distribution.

Mass-production methods are based on two principles: the use of machines in the production of standard, interchangeable parts, and the division and specialization of human labor.

Basically, the production operation is divided into specialized tasks comprised of simple, repetitive motions and minimum handling of the work. This makes the tasks easy to learn so they can be performed even by nonskilled laborers.

This results in a standardized design of the product, allowing a large run of parts that can then be fitted to the other parts with little or no adjustment needed. This is done by developing specialized machines and processes which are often patented.

Planning for Mass Production

The planning begins with the design of the product and an assessment of its market. Market estimates will help you establish the volume levels that must be produced, and the anticipated growth and fluctuations of your market.

The design of the product must conform to criteria of functionality and aesthetic appeal, while staying within the limits of standardized production. These include the materials that are most cost-efficient and readily available, and the processes used to fabricate the product.

The manner in which material will flow through the production line is particularly important. The transport of raw materials (location and availability) and purchase of preassembled components constitute the beginning of the line. The placement of manual and machine operations depends on the best way to design the tools and machines.

Then the output rate for each component of the production line is measured to prevent bottlenecks from forming.

Raw materials arriving at the plant site must be carefully coordinated with scheduled production needs, so as to reduce storage to a minimum. To eliminate storage at the other end of the production line, the finished product needs to be moved to distribution points as quickly as possible.

Pros and Cons of Mass Production

Mass production lowers costs in the long run, and not only improves the uniformity of your product but also the quality. Standardized design, materials, and processes help you monitor production and control quality without the need for detailed inspection of each product.

In fact, there is a direct correlation between the number of products manufactured and the cost per unit. The more produced, the cheaper the overall cost.

However, the volume of production must be large enough to warrant splitting the production process into a series of tasks, as well as to justify a capital investment in specialized machinery. Mass production also needs the support of technical staff and trained operators.

In addition, mass production is not very flexible. Changes in the design of your product can mean expensive changes in the production line or machinery used to manufacture the components.

Types of Mass Production

There are two basic types of mass-production facilities: continuous and batch. On the *continuous* production line, components and subassemblies pass through a series of operations and emerge at the end of the line as a completed product.

In *batch* production, a given quantity is moved as a batch

through one or more steps, and the products emerge more or less simultaneously at the end of the production line.

Many production lines combine the two methods, batch producing smaller elements (like circuits) which will then be separated and united to the rest of the product in a continuous line.

Production Rate

A production line is usually designed to operate at a certain rate. If the production levels fall below that rate, then they are being inefficiently used. If the rate is too high, operators must be paid overtime and machine maintenance suffers, causing breakdowns.

Large fluctuations in demand or increased demand must be planned into the system to keep from overloading parts of the production line. This is why working with market research and advertising can help keep the demand for your product consistent and growing.

When you are first developing and manufacturing your product, the biggest savings can be found when you turn to mass production. But this will level off as the volumes are further increased, even leading to loss of income through lack of coordination of the entire system if your production line is overloaded. Often, as demand grows, an entirely new production line must be started to handle the increase profitably.

Pilot Line

If your production line is new and untried or particularly complex, then you may want to create a *pilot line* to test the procedures. The pilot line may be a scaled down version of the production line, including the parts that are most tricky or uncertain. This will help you in the development of a full-scale production line.

Changes in product design to better suit mass-production techniques can be made at this point with less cost than retooling an entire production line. In addition, experience is gained by operators and managers during the pilot line that helps facilitate full-scale production.

Training

Your operators must be trained to perform their specialized tasks in the production line. You will also need support personnel such as equipment servicing, administration, management, and plant maintenance workers.

Normally, the production line starts up slowly, giving personnel time to see how well the line functions and make changes if necessary. As experience is gained, the process is speeded up until planned levels of output are reached.

Mass production works best when the engineering and operating personnel work together to improve productivity. Online operators inevitably discover ways to speed the process or refine normal operating procedures, and these can be incorporated into the line.

Computers

Computer simulation can be a great asset when you are planning production facilities and processes. Large quantities of data can easily be collected, analyzed, and compared. There are software programs you can buy at your local computer store to help you.

14 | *Distributing Your Product*

Once you have the finished product, you can either do the marketing and distribution yourself or you can hire an outside marketing firm to be your exclusive distributor. This means your product will be sold under the distributor's name and control, while you concentrate on the manufacturing side of production.

If you want to find a distributor, you can look under the classified ads in major newspapers. Most distributors work nationwide, advertising in trade magazines, traveling to trade shows, and doing public relations. They contact chain outlets to contract for mass distribution of your product.

This sort of cooperation can work very well. The distributor is responsible only for his office maintenance and doesn't have to deal with storage and shipping. Usually, products are shipped to the customers directly from the manufacturing facility or warehouse.

Distribution Contracts

When contracting with a distributor, the important aspects are the distributor's territory, quantity of product available, price, terms of payment, warranty, quality control, shipping arrangements, patent rights, default, and infringement. It's a complicated agreement involving rights of both manufacturer and distributor.

It's best when using a distributor to have a trademark for the product you own. This will ensure that the product is ultimately yours, not the distributor's.

Transportation

If you want to distribute to a number of retail facilities yourself, keep in mind three principles that underlie smooth operation: The best system involves minimal handling; the larger the volume handled, the lower the unit cost; products should be moved as part of a larger unit for as long as possible.

Transportation methods are best evaluated in terms of time, location, cube, weight carried, and cost.

Time refers to the hours necessary to complete a transfer of goods. Airplanes have a quick transit time, but the time it takes to unload and transfer to trucks must also be included.

Location includes the possible points to which a form of transportation can go. Trains go from one fixed point to another, while trucks can go almost anywhere.

Weight is important because the cost of transport is usually quoted in terms of cost-per-unit of weight.

Cube is the efficiency of the transport. Trucks and airplanes have cube limitations, while trains can easily add more cars. Light, bulky items will cost more per pound (like bicycles or chairs), so it can be cheaper to transport the product partially unassembled.

Cost of transport is influenced by these conditions. Generally, the heavier the loading and the higher the density (cube), the lower the cost. Costs increase with speed and the number of locations to which delivery is made.

Drop-shipping

When you ship products to many individual customers from a place other than the advertised office or production facility, it is known as drop-shipping. If you have a national distributor agreement with an individual or take orders from a mail-order catalog, then it makes sense for you to drop-ship.

This way, the distributor doesn't have to deal with retail space or warehousing the product. The manufacturer is better equipped to store the finished product for a short period of time. Then it is shipped through any of the established carriers such as United Parcel Service, DHL, United States Postal Service, etc.

It is also customary to add the price of shipping to the price per unit.

Part IV
Advertising Your Idea

15 | *Advertising: Do You Need It?*

$\mathbf{Y}$our marketing plans ideally began in conjunction with the development of your product. But once your product has been developed and manufactured, then you can incorporate the other side of marketing—advertising—to reach your potential customers.

Different kinds of businesses use advertising to motivate different kinds of markets. A retailer advertises to build store traffic and to keep regular customers informed about his goods. A manufacturer advertises to build trademark preference so customers will chose his product. The manufacturer of industrial goods, such as machinery and office equipment, advertises to other companies to use the product in their operations. Almost all business firms, whether they are retailers, manufacturers, or service institutions such as banks, airlines, and restaurants, need to advertise to build an identity as a company.

The fact that you have the opportunity to advertise gives your venture the chance to succeed. If you have a good product or service that is fairly priced, you can advertise and build on your projected market. You obviously can't match the giant firms on a national scale right away, but you can compete locally or regionally. As your business grows, you can use advertising to enter new markets and expand.

Since there is no way to accurately record the success of advertising, some economists and experts claim that advertising is wasteful. The best way to keep track of how your customers hear about you is to include that question on any customer service information you print, along with a number to call or a postage-paid postcard.

History of Advertising

Advertising began when public criers in ancient times walked through the streets calling attention to various products for sale. The oldest known written advertisement was found in Thebes and dates to 1,000 B.C. It offers a gold coin for the return of a slave.

With printing came the change from a simple announcement to a system of suggestion and argument in support of the product. Slogans and jingles became favorite advertising techniques. Some of the trademarks famous today were popularized in the nineteenth century—for example, a stylized version of the impregnable Gilbraltar became the Prudential "rock." In the twentieth century, the slogan became "It pays to advertise." Radio and television proved to be even better vehicles for advertisement than publications, and the idea of brand name image was expanded and exploited.

Now, a product or service can not only serve a basic utilitarian function, it can also provide aesthetic satisfaction through its design; or enhance its owner's status; or appeal to an unconscious desire for power, strength, desirability, etc.

Market research

Market research is essential to successful advertising, including personal selling and media advertising. You want to reach out to your market, advertising and promoting your product in a way that appeals to it most. Mass communication is impersonal unless you cater to your particular market segment, speaking in your customers' language and conforming to their taste.

Packaging

The packaging of merchandise is part of the selling effort and must be designed to appeal to the targeted market. Packaging often starts out as part of the functional design of the product or service, but it can become a symbol of the product itself—such as aerosol containers for hairspray and deodorant. Advertising relies on the recognition factor of your product.

Trademark

The trademark is used to tell your product from someone else's similar product. Like packaging, your trademark can become part of the product in the mind of the customer and should be used as a fundamental part of your advertising campaign.

Guarantee or Warranty

An important part of your company's product policy is the guarantee or warranty. As either the manufacturer or the retailer, you promise the customer certain services and performance standards. Your liability may be limited by this guarantee, while it also creates a promotional message of reliability and good customer service.

16 | *Creating Your Advertising*

When you are developing an advertising strategy, there are several questions you will want to consider. To whom should your advertising be addressed? What is the message you wish to convey? What information should the message contain? Which media do you want to use? And last, but not least—what is your budget?

To be effective, advertising needs to be aimed at a specific group of people. You need to determine the market segments that are the best prospective customers for your product and then create advertising that communicates to them in *their* language.

You want your advertising to convey a certain image, in the hope that your audience will buy your product or use your service immediately. The way you convey this message depends on the media you choose, and the tone, style, and technique of presentation. Your budget will also dictate which media you use and how and when expenditures are to be allocated to markets.

Advertising Agencies

Advertising agencies began to appear in the middle of the nineteenth century and primarily dealt with selling space in weekly newspapers and magazines. By the beginning of the twentieth century, service to the advertiser became the focus of advertising agencies. They began to plan and execute advertising campaigns.

If you don't want to make the advertising decisions yourself, the typical advertising agency is staffed to perform a variety of jobs for your company. It has expertise at planning marketing and advertising strategies; writing copy; preparing artwork, layouts, and television story boards; buying artwork and advertising space in selected media; coordinating the printing or producing commercials; researching markets, media, copy and results; and dealing with public relations, billing and paying media.

Smaller agencies usually concentrate on planning, preparing, and placing advertising.

Advertising Design

Even if you hire an advertising agency, you need to take part in the creation of the message you want to convey about your product or service. It helps if you understand the techniques behind advertising design.

Advertising design must communicate your message quickly and clearly, with the goal being to influence the audience to buy your product or service. Thus, the advertisements must do several things at once: attract attention, leave the impact of your message in the customer's conscious or unconscious mind, and induce action in your customers.

Advertising requires that your ideas be given a visual form by artistic and graphic design. New sophisticated techniques of reproducing and representing acoustic and visual material have given advertising new scope. Phototypesetting techniques can do far more than hand composition, monotype, and linotype. Many advertising displays are currently being programmed by computer.

Anything you use to promote your business can be

considered advertising: sales letters, insertions in newspapers and magazines, enclosures, prospectuses, brochures,
catalogs, leaflets, books, posters, films and slides, television
commercials, aerial advertising, billboards, shop window
displays, and exhibits. Advertising aids include packaging,
wrapping paper, book jackets, which not only identify the
product but serve as promotional material.

Each medium has its own demands. Whereas a poster is
designed to produce an effect at a distance and must be
drawn on a large scale, a newspaper advertisement has to be
designed with greater attention to details. The idea is to
achieve the maximum of clarity and impact with the
minimum resources of color and form.

Motivational Research

As with development, all of your advertising decisions
can be aided by researching your target customer. If you
understand your customer, you can influence him enough to
buy your product or use your service. Your customers
already have attitudes toward different products and new
product concepts, and they have motivations that affect
their buying behavior. Often their response is based on
society or environment, the effect of which can be studied
and analyzed. There is seldom more than one reason for
customer response.

Motivational research uses interviewing and projective
techniques such as word associations, sentence comple-
tions, and various other tests drawn from clinical psychia-
try. It was the growing use of these techniques that created a
general suspicion among consumers that advertisers could
elicit subconscious responses and manipulate customer
behavior. But it's not that simple. Even if you have the most
complete psychological data available about your prospective customers, you have to be able to convince them that it's

in their best interests to buy your product.

Motivational research is best used to determine the identity of the small proportion of the population that consumes the largest proportion of your product. For example, approximately 25 percent of all households in the U.S. buy 99 percent of prepared dog food. Once the heavy user group is isolated, you can address your advertising directly to them through the proper medium.

Usually, market segments are differentiated by demographic terms such as sex, age, income, and occupation. You can also determine information such as personality traits, geographic location, climate, ethnic groups, and lifestyle differences.

Image

One of the main jobs of advertising design is to create a particular image for your business or product. It doesn't matter if it is a unifying theme like a slogan or headline, or a unique visual identity in the pictorial content and style of advertising. When your product or service has its own image, your advertising will be more successful.

All advertising aids, from calendars to commercials to newspaper advertisements, need to have an unmistakable character that can be associated with your company. Whether it is conveyed through style, color, typography, or graphic form, each separate element works best if it works with the other forms of advertising to create an overall conception. Thus, the effect will be cumulative and will produce a clear image in the minds of the customers.

When it comes to individual pieces of advertising, the secret of good, effective design is to conceive the composition as a whole, in which form and content are interdependent and harmonious. A static composition may express rest, solidity, conservatism, security, and trust, whereas a dynamic composition can evoke aggressiveness, flexibility, youth, and energy. Colors can have symbolic significance—white for purity, blue for calm, red to represent something dynamic.

The medium you use has a great deal of influence on the effectiveness of your particular message. If full-color reproductions are needed, then magazines or posters are the best medium. New product introductions gain legitimacy from the "news" format of newspapers and radio. If you want to project a tone of authority, then advertise in professional journals.

Reach and Frequency

In choosing which medium you will use, the two basic variables are *reach* and *frequency*. Reach indicates the number of households or people exposed to the advertising in a given period of time. Frequency is the average number of times they are exposed.

These two variables are dependent on each other. It is possible to reach either more people less often or fewer people more often. When introducing a new product or trying to get new customers, the ideal is to reach as many people as possible. When your market is well defined or you are concentrating on brand loyalty, then it is better to expose a select audience more frequently.

Scheduling of advertising, such as the seasons, months, days, and hours when the ads will be seen, is also important. You need to determine when your target audience is available to view your advertising.

Budgeting

The exact contribution of advertising to sales and profits is difficult to measure. Some people even question that a relationship exists between advertising and sales. Yet it's common practice to identify the advertising budget as a percentage of sales.

The size of your advertising budget usually needs to be larger when most of the selling burden is on advertising rather than personal contact. You will also need to spend more when a new product is introduced, or when there is little difference among competing brands, or when the competition is advertising heavily. The amount of money you spend on advertising will fluctuate, depending on the stage your business is at. It is essential that you get feedback from your customers as to how they heard about your product or service.

Testing

Various techniques have been developed to test advertising ideas prior to publication or broadcast. People are exposed to the advertisement in a setting where the length of time can be controlled. *Opinion and attitude tests* involve showing alternative advertisements to a sample of people and measuring their preferences and attitudes. *Recall tests* use memory to determine the effectiveness of your advertising.

However, these types of tests contain an inherent element of artificiality because the exposure is very different from that encountered by a real customer. This means testing can be used only as a guide to customer reactions, not as a precise measurement.

To approximate reality, testing can be done in the media so that it reaches people during their normal reading, viewing, or listening. Responses are voluntary and objectively observed.

For mail-order selling, an ideal way to test the market is the *inquiry test*. Using a split run, two or more advertisements are placed in the same position in the same issue of the same publication so that matched samples of readers are exposed. Their responses are gathered by mailing a coupon that will show which advertisement was most effective to a coded address. For other types of selling, you can include a coded coupon with your advertising as a way to determine if it was seen and succeeded in motivating a response.

The most complicated test is one that runs the advertising in local markets and observes fluctuations in sales. As a control, a similar market where no advertisement has been run is checked for sales. The difference between test and control markets ought to indicate the success of the advertisement.

17 | *Advertising Media*

In the United States, radio and television draw most of their revenue from advertising. But there is no single best medium for advertising. Each medium has its own characteristics and reaches different market segments. Therefore, each must be considered in terms of how well it meets your requirements.

In print advertising, the measure of the newspaper's or magazine's value is the size of its circulation and the number of your prospective customers who read it. Research organizations measure advertising and report the composition of magazine or television or radio audiences in standard demographic terms such as age, sex, occupation, income, and family size. You can use these breakdowns to select the medium that best matches the demographics of your market.

The different advertising media are as follows: newspapers, magazines (consumer magazines, business publications, directories, professional journals), television, radio, direct mail, outdoor media (billboards, signs, posters, neon), promotional items, and dealer displays.

Newspapers

Because of their large circulation, newspapers are the most widely used advertising medium. Newspapers offer

97

something for everyone, whether it's national or local news, sports coverage, financial pages, current issues, entertainment, fashion, travel, or retail sections. Yet newspapers devote two-thirds of their space to advertising.

The newspaper is an ideal medium for most retailers. The circulation generally conforms to the local area retailers want to target. In addition, many major metropolitan papers offer zoned editions, with the circulation split into geographic areas so you can buy advertising space in only the part of the paper that is going to your trading zone.

The daily publication of newspapers facilitates the quick action promotions that most retailers look for. Pictures of the product, specifications, and prices can be included. In addition, the wide range of sizes of advertising space make it convenient to adjust cost to profit. Both small and large advertisers use newspapers to advertise profitably.

Newspapers can also be used to supplement other media advertising, to test a new product, or to concentrate effort where it is most needed, especially if competition is strong.

Magazines

Magazines also offer a wide range of advertising opportunities. General magazines serve many different population segments, offering a broad cross section of people in all parts of the nation.

More specialized magazines, such as business or sports or women's magazines, cater to the specialized interests of a particular group of consumers. The greatest number of magazines are in the business field, with publications for every industry and occupational grouping. Advertising in business magazines also prepares the ground for your salespeople.

Professional journals are read by architects, doctors, nurses, engineers—almost anyone trained to perform a service has a trade magazine they can refer to. These people are also in a position to recommend your product or service to other customers.

Television

More people spend more time with television than any other medium in the United States. During peak viewing hours on an average winter evening, over 50 percent of the households are tuned in. Viewing declines 20 percent in the summer months.

Television advertisers buy units of time: a minute, thirty seconds, twenty seconds, ten seconds, a quarter hour, a half hour, an hour, or longer. You as the advertiser may specify the time your commercial is to be broadcast; for a lower rate, you may leave the placement to the station's discretion.

Program time may be bought for exclusive sponsorship or multiple sponsorship. Exclusive sponsorship identifies the product with the program, but the advertiser pays the full cost. Multiple sponsorship allows advertisers to share the cost.

Audience Measurement

The composition and size of the television audience changes hour by hour. Men do most of their watching at night and on weekends. Preschool-age children watch more daytime television than school-age children, so caretakers watch more daytime television, too. Age groups fifty and over do more viewing than younger groups.

We know this because there are a wide variety of ways to measure television audiences. The A.C. Nielsen Company developed an Audimeter, an electronic device that is connected to all television sets in a representative sample of households. The Audimeter makes a minute-by-minute record of the time each set is turned on, the stations it is tuned to, and the length of time on each station. Every two weeks the Nielsen organization tabulates the information. However, the Audimeter can only tell the tuning of the set, it can't record which family members are watching or how many.

The telephone polling method consists of calling a sample of households, asking if a television is turned on, and if so, which station it is turned to and who is watching. This method is relatively inexpensive and is used extensively in local market areas.

Personal interviews can be conducted in public spaces like shopping malls, with a list of TV stations or programs which individuals can check if they recall watching at a certain time of day. This method is also useful for surveying customers at specific retail sites.

There are different sets of surveys that measure television audiences in certain ways: *Program rating* tracks the percentage of households tuned to a particular program; *share-of-audience* is the percentage of households using television tuned to each program; *projected-audience* is the estimated number of households reached by a program; *audience-composition* offers a breakdown by sex, age, family size, income, etc.

Commercials

Television commercials and other kinds of film provide many different options when it comes to creating unique advertising.

A copywriter for a television commercial develops the message idea and draws on visual, aural, and optical elements to convey the theme. In much the same way a scriptwriter works, the copywriters (often a writer and artist) develop the plot, visualize the scenes, plan the action, and write instructions to the producers, actors, and technicians.

A storyboard is an illustrated script of the commercial and is used to obtain management approval and to facilitate production.

If the tape consists of live action, titles, subtitles, and possibly functional diagrams and statistics must be designed in addition to the movie set. If the film is animated, any type of drawing can be used, from fairy-tale cartoons to surrealistic montage, and in any style, including naturalism, simplified, stylized, abstract, and symbolic, depending on what best illustrates your message and product.

It's important that only one or two ideas be in the picture frame at the same time during a commercial; otherwise the pictorial ideas will become confused. Colors and their sequences are also important, and lettering styles and images must compliment one another. Therefore, the designer must work closely with the producer, the copywriter, and the cameraman.

Radio

Radio advertising is sold much the same way television time is, and the same methods of audience measurement are used. However, radio audiences are not measured as frequently or as extensively by regular surveys. Radio is also primarily a local medium, so retailers account for about two-thirds of all radio advertising expenditures.

Creating commercials for radio is much easier than for television. Usually, you can hire the stations DJs to make a recording of your commercial; that way you know you have a built-in audience that is receptive to the person making the pitch.

Direct Mail

You can send your advertising directly to individual prospects by mail. The message can take one of many forms:

letter, folder, booklet, brochure, post card, catalog, or coupons.

In the letter form, the message can be personalized by addressing the recipient by name, by appealing to his personal concerns, and by using the language and style of a personal letter. The message will be read at least partly by most of the recipients, and you know it will be read on the date received.

Using direct mail, you can single out special groups for special needs by buying or renting mailing lists. The mailing list is the critical factor in direct-mail advertising. Frequently used sources of names and addresses can be found in telephone and city directories, trade directories, professional directories, commercial rating books, tax lists, club membership lists, and mailing lists compiled by other retailers.

You can check your local Yellow Pages for local companies that make a business of compiling lists and selling them to advertisers.

Billboards

Printed posters and billboards are the most important types of outdoor media. The standard poster or billboard is located on heavily traveled routes, including station posters that reach millions of public transportation riders each day.

The typical billboard provides brief exposure to motorists and must convey a message that can be seen or read at a glance. A single, simple visual idea with a caption is usually most appropriate. This prevents the use of billboards when it comes to communicating information regarding specifications, pricing, etc.

There are various styles you can use with posters and billboards. The illustrative style presents the theme or object with an atmospheric appeal. The realistic style provides objective information through its copy and rendering of the product. The constructionist style arranges pictorial elements in accordance with their thematic importance. The experimental style surprises the viewer in the novel way it presents its message or in the message itself.

Signs

In lettered signs on doors, windows, and buildings, you must make sure of three things: The lettering must be visible at a certain distance; the sign must make an impact by its style and originality; it must be integrated with the architecture in size, form, color, and material.

If the sign is to be visible at night, you can chose between neon lettering and spotlighted signs. With neon, the shape must conform to certain technical requirements.

In composing lettered signs on the sides of delivery vans, trucks, or cars, you must take into account the movement of the vehicle. The letters need to be spaced so they won't run together when read. High contrast, such as a dark color on white or pale color, makes reading easier.

Directional signs can also become part of your advertisement campaign. Signs at airports, train stations, public transportation, and even signs within your company directing people to administration or purchasing can be used as advertisement. They should conform to the image you have created in style, color, and lettering.

Dealer Displays

Dealer displays reach customers at the point of purchase, serving as a reminder or invitation to buy. These usually consist of a cardboard display stand that holds brochures or flyers advertising a certain product or service.

Promotional Items

Promotional items are useful items that are imprinted with your business or product's name. These sorts of advertising specialties are limited only by your imagination. Some of the more common items include calendars, matchbooks, lighters, key chains, memo pads, datebooks, glassware, ashtrays, notebooks, pens and pencils, toys and decorative items. Since these items are frequently used, they serve as frequent reminders of your product or service.

These items can be distributed year-round or at particular times of the year. The effectiveness of the item depends on its functional quality. If the workmanship or beauty of the object is exceptional, then your customers will keep the item in view and will be reminded of your product or service. However, if the lettering of your advertisement is so intrusive as to be annoying, the item will be discarded.

Therefore, it is very important to be guided by aesthetic considerations when placing the name of your company or product and additional information on promotional items. This information can be stamped directly on the item in plain sight or on the botton, or it can be affixed with a label. Association can be made through the style and color of the item rather than labeling. Or a more decorative rendition of your brand name can be used.

Part V
Expansion

18 | *Franchising*

Franchising is a form of business practice that accounts for approximately one-third of all retail sales in the United States. If you have an established business on which to base your accounting and franchising proposal, then it is likely that you are eligible for offering franchises.

In franchising, your degree of involvement is much higher than with licensing. Whereas your interest in the licensee's operations is usually limited to royalty payments and maximizing returns on the product, as a franchiser you are likely to be much more involved in the business aspects of running the franchise. Therefore, the franchiser retains a great deal of control over the franchise because of his ownership rights.

Regulations

Franchising is heavily regulated by the government. A Federal Trade Commission "Trade Regulation Rule" requires that, at the first personal meeting, a prospective franchisee must be provided with a complete disclosure statement, containing some twenty different categories of information. In addition, some states have their own franchise laws that require registration of the proposed sale of a franchise and a disclosure by the prospective franchisee through the means of a Uniform Franchise Offering Circular.

Franchising Contract

The important aspects of the franchising agreement are the franchiser's territory, price, terms of payment, warranty, quality control, consulting arrangements, trademark licensing, and more. It's a complicated agreement involving established rights of both the franchiser and the franchisee.

Franchising Rights

The most important right involved in franchising is the use of the trademark. Other rights are considered system licenses associated with the trademark, such as methods of doing distribution, accounting, inventory management, trade dress, and building designs. Usually these systems are set forth in a confidential operating manual used by the franchisee for the duration of the franchise.

Since the rights involved in franchising are so complex, a franchising lawyer is needed for the drafting of the documents involved in establishing the franchise relationship. You can locate franchise lawyers in the Business-to-Business directory or Yellow Pages.

19 | *Public Stock Offering*

When you make a public stock offering, you are selling part of your business's equity, through an underwriter, to many small investors. An underwriter is a financial firm which "buys" a block of stock from you to sell to their customers, who become your stockholders. You, in turn, receive an infusion of capital to be used for expansion.

One of the main tasks of your lawyer will be to negotiate the price per share. The underwriter will want the price low, while you want it as high as possible without risking a downturn in price soon after the initial offering. Also key is the volume of shares to be traded in the over-the-counter (OTC) market.

Is your company ready to go public? There are certain standards set by the New York Stock Exchange that you must meet, but the unwritten rule of thumb on Wall Street is that a company is ready to go public when it has a million dollars in profits on ten million dollars in sales. If your business hasn't reached that stage, it's best to raise capital privately.

The Stock Market

It's best to consider the condition of the stock market before making a public offering. Most small companies trade their stock in the over-the-counter market, also known as the Pink Sheets. You can determine the success of companies in your field by following their progress in the Pink Sheets.

If you decide to sell stock, you need to get an underwriter to properly register your company. This move includes full disclosure of the financial state of your company. Under the Securities Act of 1933, it is against the law to sell or promote stock before it is properly registered. If you are caught selling or promoting unregistered stock, you can destroy your offering and possibly your company.

The Underwriter

The underwriter will select the best form of public offering depending on your financial needs and the condition of the stock market. Many underwriters specialize in certain business fields, so find one that suits your company.

Underwriters are paid directly, in stock, or in options for lower stock prices in the future. The SEC has rules regarding the number of investors you can show your deal to, so submit your business plan to one underwriter at a time. Wait for a reply before moving to your next choice.

The Underwriting Proposal

Like any business plan, your underwriting proposal is a selling tool. Emphasize the uniqueness of your company and product, including full disclosure on the history of your company, your current financial statement, and the prospects of your company in its particular field.

The following is an outline of a typical underwriting proposal:

I. *The Company*
    A. Description of company
        1. Date and state of incorporation

      2. Principal stockholders

      3. Capital structure

      4. Location

II. *The Management*

    A. Resumes of key executives and officers of the company

    B. Employment contracts with key executives

III. *The Product*

    A. Production

    B. Customer Profile

IV. *The Competition*

    A. Similar publicly held companies

    B. Growth potential of your company

Pricing Your Stock

The price of your stock is determined by the underwriter's evaluation of the company. The statistics of your company are compared with those from similar companies, particularly those that have already gone public. The underwriter tries to forecast the future earnings-per-share of your company.

The underwriter also takes into account your intended purpose with the capital. If it is for expansion, construction, and production improvement, increased revenues are indicated. If it is just to increase working capital or pay old debt, the underwriter takes into account the fact that your company's sales will remain at current volume.

Eligibility

Your company must meet certain qualifications before you can publicly sell stock. The New York Stock Exchange generally requires the following minimums for Initial Listing:

1. Demonstrated earning power under competitive
   conditions of $2.5 million before income taxes for
   the most recent year and $2 million pretax for
   each of the two preceding years
2. Net tangible assets of $16 million
3. A total of $16 million in market value of publicly
   held stock
4. A total of one million common shares publicly
   held
5. Two thousand holders of 100 shares or more of
   common stock.

In addition, other qualifications are considered, such as:
the degree of national interest in the company; its relative
position and stability in the industry; and whether it is in
an expanding industry with prospects of at least maintaining its relative position.

Advantages of Public Offering

If your small business can barely meet the requirements
of going public, should you do it? Here's a list of a few of the
advantages.

Additional Capital

If your company needs money for long-term expansion,
then a public sale of equity may be the best answer. Short-
term loans can strain cash flow. Equity is permanent
capital, and in certain situations, may be cheaper than debt.

Acquiring Loans

Banks are more willing to lend to publicly held companies at more favorable terms. This is because every aspect
of your company is on public record, with daily updates in
the form of "over-the-counter" quotes of stock prices.

Repayment of Loans

If your company is successful in going public and the after-market price of your stock is above the initial offering price, then your equity structure is considered sound. It is then easier to renegotiate loan repayments.

Disadvantages of Public Offering

As a publicly held company, you have to adhere to specific regulations that ensure public security. Your own corporation bylaws must be strictly followed, as well as SEC regulations. You have to consider your stockholders in every major decision, so this leads to bureaucratic red tape.

Since you have to please the stockholders, who will carefully follow the rise and fall of their dividends, you will be under pressure as to how you run your company. Inherently, you lose some, if not most, of your control over your company.

Index